CHicKS Dig fries

...s you need to remember!

Love
Amanda
(XX)

CHICKS Dig fries

A GUIDE for CLUELESS MEN

Written & illustrated By Bob Mathews

Andrews McMeel Publishing

Kansas City

CHiCKS DiG FRieS

ISBN: 0-7407-3851-8

Library of Congress Control Number: 2003101150

03 04 05 06 07 WKT 10 9 8 7 6 5 4 3 2 1

Dedicated to

 Lisa
&
Heidi,

the two women I've loved . . .
and lost.

Because I wasn't smart enough
to take my own advice.

INTRODUCTION

After years and years of dating,
even the most hapless moron (such as
myself) eventually learns a thing or two
despite himself.

Here's what I've learned . . .

Women are soft, they smell good, they
have cute giggles, and we men want
them. And it's really not so tough to
please them and make them feel special.
The first step is knowing what they like,
and everyone knows that chicks do,
in fact, dig fries.

CHICKS DIG
Fries

You got it . . . french fries.
With honey mustard or
plain old ketchup on the side—
it doesn't matter. Chicks dig fries.

Helpful Hint:

Whatever you do, don't tell her that
they're fattening . . . and keep your fingers
out of reach.

CHICKS DiG
Cats

Why? Who knows? They just do.
If you despise the wretched creature
(the cat, I mean) try to be mean to it
only when she's not looking.
Actually, win the cat's affection
and you'll probably win hers.

CHICKS DIG

a GUY WHO Makes a BIG DeaL OUT OF Her BirtHDaY

The ultimate, of course, is a vacation, but that's often too expensive or impractical. Anything you dream up will most likely be appreciated, as long as you give it ample thought. Plan ahead for this.

CHICKS DIG
Horses

I don't know why, exactly; they just do.

CHICKS DIG

CHIPS & SALSA

Just like with the fries,
don't tell her that
they're fattening.

CHICKS DIG

Flannel

You can't go wrong.
Right out of
an old classic movie.

CHiCKS DiG
Manicures, pedicures, & Facials

They make her feel pampered.

HELPFUL HiNT:
Great as a gift certificate.

CHICKS DIG
SOAPS, SHAMPOOS, & Conditioners

Maybe a bar of cheap soap is fine for your entire body and hair, but it doesn't fit the bill for her. Selecting a decent product for her will make her happy and show how thoughtful you are. Or better yet, wash her hair for her and she's putty in your hands.

Helpful Hint:

A gift certificate to a salon or spa is a nice, easy compromise. If done over the phone, it requires little effort on your part.

CHICKS DIG
Convertibles

If you own one you're lucky. Never sell it.
Women love 'em! And they open up a
whole world of possibilities when it
comes to car sex!

CHICKS DiG
Hard Butts

Try some lunges or squats.
Size doesn't matter,
it just has to be hard.

(Pun intended.)

CHICKS DIG

Dancing

You don't have to be good.
Just do it.

If you're clueless on the dance floor,
just watch other guys dancing nearby and copy them;
no one will ever know.

CHiCKS DiG
Romantic Movies

Maybe martial arts and explosions are the ticket for you, but give her a break.

Try <u>Pretty Woman,</u> <u>Roman Holiday,</u> <u>Sleepless in Seattle,</u> or the like.

CHICKS DIG

Rearranging the Furniture

There is absolutely no point to this whatsoever, but keep in mind— she seems to really care about it.

HELPFUL HINT:

It's a cheap, easy fix and it beats having to buy new stuff.

CHICKS DIG

Fabrics, Linens, & Other Materials

Allow her a moment and you can shop
the electronics section in peace.

CHICKS DIG

Car Washes &
Oil Changes

Actually they don't dig 'em,
but they love it if you do it for them,
or take their car in and have it done.

Might as well fill 'er up while you're out and about.

CHICKS DIG

GUYS WHO Aren't Susceptible to Road Rage

We share the road; calm down.

CHICKS DiG
GUYS WHO Can COOK

It's really not her job.
Share the load.

CHICKS DIG

OUtfits and/or SHOes as a Gift

If you haven't a clue, try browsing through ads in any issue of a "chick" magazine. Well-dressed mannequins in stores also provide good ideas.

Make sure to ask for a "gift receipt" so she can exchange them later. She's sure to hate what you got her. But you still have to try.

CHICKS DIG

CANDLES & BUBBLE BATHS

Let's face it, everything and everyone looks better by candlelight.

And a bubble bath makes her feel feminine.

CHICKS DIG
POPCORN

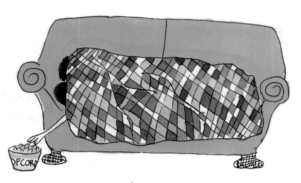

If you're sitting at home watching
a rented movie, making popcorn detracts
attention from the fact that you've only
spent about five bucks on this date.
Plus you got her on a couch—
what more do ya want?

CHICKS DIG

Being Called by a Nickname

If you don't have one for her,
just make one up. Calling her by her
middle name isn't bad either.

HELPFUL HINT:

"Honey-bunny" and "Baby" are taken.

CHiCKS DiG
wine

CLICK

Most women love wine. If you're a
beer kind of guy, just try wine once
in a while. It seems classier.

CHICKS DIG
Kissing

Preferably soft and for a long time.
Allow her to lose the desire to kiss you
and she may just lose you too one day.

CHICKS DIG
SHAVED FACES

Some women like facial hair,
but most women like a soft,
clean-shaven face to kiss.

CHICKS DIG
A GUY WHO MAKES A BIG DEAL OUT OF THE HOLIDAYS

-Argh-h

It's not that hard, ya Scrooge!
You don't need a lot of money to
make it special.

CHICKS DiG
Big, Stupid, Ugly, Flowery Hats

Despite the fact that only a few
women can pull it off, try to indulge
her occasionally.

CHICKS DIG

Baskets

Whatever it is, put it in a basket.
It's all in the presentation.

CHICKS DiG
THE THEATER

It feels like a real night out.

CHICKS DIG

A GUY WHO WILL SHARE THE At-Home WORKLOAD

Dishes, the garbage, laundry, etc.
Who wants to live like a pig, anyhow?

HELPFUL HINT:

The fifteen minutes of work will save you an hour
of arguing about it.

CHICKS DIG
Going Out for Dinner

It doesn't have to be expensive,
just a place where the two of you can
stare at each other across a table
of dishes that neither of you
has to wash.

CHICKS DIg
a GUY WHO PAYS

In this case, "no" most likely means "yes."

CHICKS DIG
BACK RUBS

oh-h-h-h lucky me

It's a nice way to get her to remove her top. If that's not an issue, then it's always nice ammo later: "Well, I always rub your back, don't I?"

CHICKS DIG
BUTT RUBS

This is a win-win situation. They also like their legs and feet rubbed (those are the things below their butt that they stand on).

CHICKS DIG
HEAD RUBS

Who doesn't?

CHICKS DIG
DIAMOND JEWELRY

Whether it's earrings, a bracelet,
a necklace, or a ring, she'd most likely
prefer it if it was picked out by you
and given as a surprise.

HELPFUL Hint:

Her girlfriend or sister could help you
secretly pick it out, unless they're so cute
as to cause a problem.

CHICKS DIG
Getting Their Hair Brushed

Makes her feel pampered.

You can watch TV or talk on the phone as you do this.

CHICKS DiG
BOiLED WATER

Whether you're making tea or hot chocolate, women want the water boiled, not microwaved.

CHICKS DIG
GUYS WHO CAN PLAY A MUSICAL INSTRUMENT

Show her your "artistic" side,
even if you suck.

CHICKS DIG
BALLOON RIDES

And other such romantic notions.

CHICKS DIG
OLD-FASHIONED GUYS

I.e., Polite.

CHICKS DiG
"JUST BECAUSE" SURPRISES

Surprise dinners made by you are nice,
making the bed yourself works,
and flowers and cards are
always winners.

Helpful Hint:

Flowers or gifts must be delivered to her where others
can witness and therefore be adequately jealous.

CHICKS DIG

A GUY WHO'S NICE TO HER FRIENDS AND FAMILY

Even if you're faking it.
(See "Chicks Dig Cats.")

CHICKS DIG

scones

Probably because we don't even know what they are. They're like really hard doughnuts, right?

CHICKS DIG
CHOCOLATE

Of course we all knew this one,
but the fancier and more expensive
the better.

CHICKS DIG
coffee

Again, fancy and expensive.
A small price to pay to make her happy.

CHICKS DIG

POTPOURRI

It smells good, so why not?

CHICKS DiG
a GOOD SPort

Shopping with them and not
making it a miserable experience
is a good example.

CHICKS DiG
a GOOD Listener

Even if what she's saying is totally absurd, nonsensical, and boring. Sometimes a woman just wants to tell you what's on her mind and doesn't want your know-it-all opinion in return.

Helpful Hint:

Faking listening is easier than faking concerned conversation anyhow.

CHICKS DIG
ATHLETIC GUYS

You don't have to be a
pro ball player, just get up off
the couch once in a while.

chicks dig

pillows

& comforters

Tons of 'em! The more the merrier.
If you're lucky, she'll snuggle you
and not a pillow.

And maybe we don't care or even
know what a duvet cover is or does,
but they all do. Indulge her.

CHICKS DIG
SHARP-DRESSED MEN

Maybe your job and lifestyle don't require it, but when you get home try leaving your dirty sweats in the hamper.

CHICKS DIG
GUYS WHO DON'T SMOKE

The only person to ever look cool
smoking was Humphrey Bogart in
the old black-and-white movies.
Guess what?
You ain't Bogey!

CHICKS DiG
BELTS

They like the "complete" accessorized look, and I think they like the sound when they're coming off.

When it's done nicely and in fun.

CHICKS DiG
GUYS WHO DON'T ALWAYS Talk about sex

We men may understand that everything in life is just some form of foreplay, but let's not tell the womenfolk. Slow down, and hopefully you'll get there eventually.

CHICKS DIG
GUYS WHO SMELL GOOD

If you're one of those guys who thinks he doesn't need deodorant, trust me—you're only kidding yourself. They're talking about you behind your back.

CHICKS DIG

LULLabies

The worse your voice,
the sweeter the moment.

They use them for all kinds of makeup things. If you're a single guy hoping she'll spend the night, having cotton balls around could be the deal maker.

A blow dryer and a new toothbrush are good, too.

CHICKS DIg
Lotion

A quality lotion as a stocking stuffer
works great for her.

HELPFUL HINT:

Applying it to her works great for you.

CHICKS DIG
SUNSHINE

Sunny breakfast nooks or sun-drenched beaches—doesn't matter.
A sunny day makes a girl happy.

Bring a small tub of it with one spoon into the bedroom afterward, and she'll think she found the perfect man.

You can't win with this one.

CHICKS DIG
GUYS WHO WILL MAKE a Sacrifice

If you can record the big game or Britney's live concert and watch it later, it'll make her day.

I know it's difficult. Lying comes so naturally, but try really hard.

CHICKS DIG
Free-Spirited Men

As long as you're not so free that you can't manage to pay the rent on time.

Stop whatever it is you're doing,
because whatever it is, it's wrong.
Women like it when we do the opposite
of what we're doing now.

CHICKS DIG

LOYALTY & Commitment

If you break her trust, you may never get it back. Women like a guy they can trust. In short, they like a guy who acts like a man.

CHICKS DIG
Being Happy

When she's not happy, you probably won't be either. Remember, it's a woman's world; we're just here for the ride.

Think you know what

CHiCKS DiG ?

Care to share?

Submit your insight and help millions
of men in the struggle to learn
more about the fairer sex.

Go to

CHiCKS DiG
fries.COM